John Montague

THE IRISH WRITERS SERIES
James F. Carens, General Editor

EIMAR O'DUFFY	Robert Hogan
J. C. MANGAN	James Kilroy
J. M. SYNGE	Robin Skelton
PAUL VINCENT CARROLL	Paul A. Doyle
SEAN O'CASEY	Bernard Benstock
SEUMAS O'KELLY	George Brandon Saul
SHERIDAN LEFANU	Michael Begnal
SOMERVILLE AND ROSS	John Cronin
STANDISH O'GRADY	Phillip L. Marcus
SUSAN L. MITCHELL	Richard M. Kain
W. R. RODGERS	Darcy O'Brien
MERVYN WALL	Robert Hogan
LADY GREGORY	Hazard Adams
LIAM O'FLAHERTY	James O'Brien
MARIA EDGEWORTH	James Newcomer
SIR SAMUEL FERGUSON	Malcolm Brown
BRIAN FRIEL	D. E. S. Maxwell
PEADAR O'DONNELL	Grattan Freyer
DANIEL CORKERY	George Brandon Saul
BENEDICT KIELY	Daniel Casey
CHARLES ROBERT MATURIN	Robert E. Lougy
DOUGLAS HYDE	Gareth Dunleavy
EDNA O'BRIEN	Grace Eckley
FRANCIS STUART	J. H. Natterstad
JOHN BUTLER YEATS	Douglas N. Archibald
JOHN MONTAGUE	Frank Kersnowski
KATHARINE TYNAN	Marilyn Gaddis Rose
BRIAN MOORE	Jeanne Flood
PATRICK KAVANAGH	Darcy O'Brien
OLIVER ST. JOHN GOGARTY	J. B. Lyons
GEORGE FITZMAURICE	Arthur McGuinness

GEORGE RUSSELL (AE)	Richard M. Kain and James H. O'Brien
IRIS MURDOCH	Donna Gerstenberger
MARY LAVIN	Zack Bowen
FRANK O'CONNOR	James H. Matthews
ELIZABETH BOWEN	Edwin J. Kenney, Jr.
WILLIAM ALLINGHAM	Alan Warner
SEAMUS HEANEY	Robert Buttel
THOMAS DAVIS	Eileen Sullivan

JOHN MONTAGUE

Frank Kersnowski

Lewisburg

BUCKNELL UNIVERSITY PRESS

London: **ASSOCIATED UNIVERSITY PRESSES**

© 1975 by Associated University Presses, Inc.

Associated University Presses, Inc.
Cranbury, New Jersey 08512

Associated University Presses
108 New Bond Street
London W1Y OQX, England

Library of Congress Cataloging in Publication Data

Kersnowski, Frank L   1934-
John Montague.

   (The Irish writers series)
   Bibliography: p.
   1. Montague, John—Criticism and interpretation.
PR6063.05Z8   821'.9'14   78-168811
ISBN O-8387-7807-0
ISBN 0-8387-7983-2 (pbk.)

For Maud

The research for this study was made possible by grants from Trinity University, San Antonio, Texas, and The National Endowment for the Humanities.

Printed in the United States of America

Contents

Chronology

1929	Born in Brooklyn, New York.
1933	Moved to County Tyrone, Northern Ireland, to live with his father's sisters on their farm.
1934-40	Attended Garvaghey and Glencull Primary Schools.
1940-45	Attended St. Patrick's College, Armagh.
1945-53	Attended University College, Dublin. M.A. in Anglo-Irish Literature.
1949-52	Film critic and literary correspondent, Irish Catholic paper.
1953-54	Fulbright Scholar at Yale Graduate School.
1954-55	Joined in Writer's Workshop, University of Iowa.
1955-56	Taught at University of California, Berkeley.

1956   Married.

1956-60   Editor in Bord Failte, Irish Tourist Board. Lived in Dublin.

1961   Moved to Paris.

1961-64   Paris Correspondent of *The Irish Times*

1964-65   In Poetry Workshop, University of California, Berkeley.

1967-68   Taught at University College, Dublin.

1969-70   Taught at the Experimental University of Vincennes.

1972   Taught at University College, Cork.

1973   Still there.

John Montague

1
Introduction

The Irish Literary Renaissance has rightfully assumed such importance in this century that critics have difficulty appraising the Irish writers who come after it since these later writers often seem to be copies of their elders or to be lesser. Understandably, the contemporary Irish writer has often been abrupt in dismissing the immediate past and outspoken in proclaiming the significance of his own identity as a writer. The most important organ of post-Renaissance beliefs was *Envoy,* a periodical guided by Patrick Kavanagh, Anthony Cronin, and John Ryan, who seemed determined to commit the Literary Renaissance to the earth. All shared belief in the necessity of an internationalist literature, and self-consciously Irish writing seldom appeared.

John Montague came to Dublin during the internationalists' attack and growth, and at this time he discovered his own ability as a poet. Understandably, he often wrote in the new mode. Exile was a frequent theme. But beginning to show even in his first volume,

Forms of Exile, is his concern with an identity as poet that can be productive and comfortable in several cultures. Unlike many of his contemporaries, however, John Montague did not, even in his first volume, refuse to consider the significance of Ireland to himself as man and writer. And in this respect, as well as in later poetic innovations, he preceded much that has happened in contemporary Irish literature.

His concern with Ireland has been a constant, though not single, theme. Recently, he has written about the civil rights struggle in Ulster and in 1972 returned to Ireland as a lecturer at University College, Cork. Since his identity as a writer has been shaped by the years he has lived in France and in the United States, he seems quite likely to continue writing with multicultural concerns. He increasingly looks for structures of belief and action which underlie and could unite seemingly diverse cultures. While he has not attempted to retell ancient legends and has not put traditional Irish heroes and gods into modern dress, myth, particularly in his later work, has provided him with the most basic structures of thought and art.

2

Forms of Exile

Forms of Exile, though published in 1958, shows the temper of the early 50s, as well as the early development of John Montague's poetry. The first, and larger, part of this first volume consists of almost unqualified rejection of Ireland. The subjects, though, are not those of Yeats; for the young man who wrote these poems had, at that time, only a bookish familiarity with the Anglo-Irish. To a quite unsurprising extent, the book is priest-ridden. Some of the best, and most controversial, of the poems concern the debilitating effect of the Church on life in Ireland. "A Footnote on Monasticism: Dingle Peninsula," written by 1953, presents an old ruined monastery and then musingly recreates the past as the poet imagines himself one of these silent, worshipful men:

> anchorites whose love of God
> Was selfishly alone, a matter so great
> That only to stone could they whisper it . . . .

Like many other young Irishmen of his time, John Montague, though never coerced by his family, was encouraged to consider a vocation. Perhaps for that reason, these early poems so often speak from the persona of the priest.

"Soliloquy on a Southern Strand," completed after Montague's return to Ireland in 1956, examines another part of a priest's life: the end when he must sum up his achievement. The poem is spoken by an old priest as he sits on a beach in Australia and thinks back to his youth in Ireland. A country boy, he had been shy, somewhat inept. So in school with the more sophisticated, he willingly accepted the security offered by the cloth. After years of continence, he has come to a slow and gentle life surrounded by young sun-worshipers who must consider him alien and irrelevant. He himself finds scant more significance in his life:

No martyrdom, no wonder, no real loss, . . .

The contrast in this poem is between vital life in a young, active culture and one that meditates on a dying past.

Several more poems he wrote after his return to Ireland contrast Irish life with that of another country. In "Rome, Anno Santo" the bleakness of Ireland forms a small dark cloud in the splendor of Rome, the harshness of Irish pilgrims contrasted with the humanism of Rome. Still the Church is not condemned, only Irish Catholicism. In "Song of the Lonely Bachelor" and even in a poem called "Prodigal Son" Montague condemns the Jansenist-charged Catholicism of Ireland for allowing the people no more than a slow telling out of beads.

Though distinctly Roman Catholic in many of the

poems, Montague does not deny the importance of the
Anglo-Irish past to him. In a series of poems written
before the trip to the United States, he alludes to a
series by Yeats with his title: "Rhetorical Meditations
in Time of Peace." Rhetorical diction, rather than
Montague's later conversational one, indicates his
following Yeats, the Anglo-Irish and English tradition.
The progress of diction in this tradition may well be
toward the language that men speak, but the men who
speak usually have a most uncolloquial choice of words.
Even in the final ominously despairing section of his
poem, Montague's words soothe the reader rather than
involve him in the grit of the experience:

> At times, we turn in most ordinary weakness and trembling
> From the sweet incense rising, the gentle light falling
> On damp slum tenement and holy mountain . . . .

This seems pallid enough when put beside Yeats.

One must, however, remember that Montague was
twenty-three when he wrote this poem. His first real
interest in poetry had begun at U.C.D. when he was
about seventeen and had been molded by Hopkins (the
birth and bane of so many Roman Catholic poets) and
then by Yeats and the Literary Revival. One of the most
basic difficulties for the Northern poet is that for him
and for almost everyone else until recently, Irish poetry
has meant that written in Southern Ireland. A young
man, such as John Montague, would be sent to U.C.D. if
he showed interest or ability in the arts. There he
would, in his writing, replace referrents of the self he
had always had with ones of Georgian Dublin, the values
of which had been pretty well set by the time he came
along.

Some writers from the North remained within the bounds of decorum, neglecting the wildness of the later Yeats, and wrote in words appropriate to the Shelbourne lounge, which with its hotel has been the center of the Anglo-Irish society for more than a century. But even in the early writing of Montague, the colloquial was heard. The very early "A Footnote on Monasticism: Dingle Peninsula" begins, "In certain places, still surprisingly, you come/ Upon them, resting like old straw hats set down/ Beside the sea. . . ." Quite likely, his interest in a conversational diction was increased by his visit to the United States.

Whether or not Montague matured into his own style during the three years he was in the United States or whether he expanded his understanding of poetry by meeting poets from another tradition seems inconsequential. He did, however, meet Robert Bly and W.D. Snodgrass at Iowa and Allen Ginsburg and Snyder at Berkeley. Though few, the poems he wrote about this period indicate a new understanding of poetry. Even "Soliloquy on a Southern Strand" has a glitter to it not found in the earlier poems. The glitter in the poems specifically about the United States, however, is that of a sloganed world, as in "Downtown, America":

NEWS OF THE LATEST TRIAL—THE
WINNING HORSE—TROOPS HAVE LANDED—COMMISSION'S
REPORT IS THROUGH
These are normal things and set the heart at rest.

Intending to condemn the brashness of the culture, Montague in his quotations has considerably expanded the technique of his poetry by including the brash, colloquial writing of the journalist. In later poems, such as *The Bread God,* the technique will return to add complexity to more mature poems.

In a three–poem sequence called "American Landscapes," he again used a quotation: "A loud-speaker car drones through the streets,/ Calling JOIN THE U.S. MARINES." but the poem itself becomes part of the gentle rhetoric he used so well. In the last two poems here he evokes the particular in all its brash and futile urgency. "Bus Stop in Nevada" gives our mobile culture to us with smell and sound:

> in a sullen cafeteria,
> Percolators hiss and cheap pies line the glass.
> Hands ply the glittering cranks of slot machines . . .

In the last poem, "Hollywood and Vine," a nearly brutal life tears through the fabric of Montague's trained poetic with force comparable to "Downtown, America." Young men solicit on the street:

> To girls stuttering past, aloof on high heels,
> Lost in gales of laughter,
> In their own awkwardness suddenly angular,
> They answer with a forced look back,
> Pivoting nervously to the cats' call of love.

Though slanted, these poems do not tell the reader how to react; and the young poet himself seems a bit unsure of how he should react.

At the back of his mind are centuries of conditioned moral responses and a weight of cultural/literary tradition that must regard what he sees in the United States as worth only censure. In Europe, the centuries have established a hierarchy of art and life, neither of which has often enough had much relevance for the majority of the population. In "Cultural Center" Montague views a mixture of Roman sculpture, Mexican sculpture, Japanese and Renaissance painting, and a Catalan crucifix. However, Montague has moments of disloyalty to his European structure, compared with which the varied assortment in an American museum seems so vital. Here the frenzy of life has not atrophied; but he is led to find a center in the melange just as is a nun who leads her class through the rooms to "the lean accusing, Catalan crucifix." The death-seeking impetus of so much Christianity still touches the young Montague.

Also he has yet to decide whether to let the colloquial increase its importance in his poetry or to pursue the more rhetorical mode of the past. No poem in *Forms of Exile* attempts to solve all these problems. After the brash newness of the United States, Montague returned to Ireland, consciously looking for the past. Six months after returning, he wrote "The Sean Bhean Vocht," which shows he is aware answers exist to his problems. In this poem he confronts the ancient figure of Ireland "Wrapped in a cocoon of rags and shawls" as she will often reappear to him: a superstitious old woman, terrifying to the young because of her ugliness and uncleanness. Her memory, though, is of distinctly Roman Catholic ways and past them of the people who spoke her language long before Christianity came to Ireland.

When he wrote this poem in 1956, Montague could not without qualification accept the past which he had only been able to piece together from pieces of flotsam like this old woman. Yet he was drawn to see what part of himself answered when the past called:

> I strode through golden light
> To the ogham script of the burial stone: . . .

But beneath the whorls of the guardian stone
What faery queen lay dust?

Though knowing little at this time of either Jung or the history of ancient Ireland, Montague readily acknowledged that past as alive in him and communicatable to others in the present through a persona. The immediate effect on his verse is to increase attention to specific details and to increase the colloquial even to the extent of quoting Irish, something rarely done by the strongly internationalist poets in the mid-50s. These techniques had been apparent even in the quite traditional poems written before the trip to the United States and were dominant in the poems written about that trip. But in "The Sean Bhean Vocht," the two approaches find their best amalgamation. Over one-third of the poem is dialogue, and the rest is tightly structured colloquial speech.

3
Poisoned Lands

Poisoned Lands, Montague's second volume, shows a further investigation into poetic forms. Dominant, however, is the sound and attitude of poetry from the fifties: elegance, irony, compression, and formal eloquence. More often than in *Forms of Exile,* the sound of local idiom appears, shattering the carefully wrought forms. Or a savagely ironic ending will make paradoxical what had been a cleanly rhetorical poem. Montague's willingness to try new forms and his need to investigate his own culture could have led him to resurrect the regionalist poetry of the nineteenth century, but Ireland remained for him one culture of many, and art became the means to view the undying forms of the past latent in the present.

The necessities of publishing partially mutilated the structure of the book as Montague had planned it, but the three parts are still evident: country, sickness, healing. Although most of them are new, several of the very good poems earlier appeared in *Forms of Exile.* The ones from that volume which were not reprinted also serve to illustrate the shape of *Poisoned Lands*. None of the American poems appeared, probably because this volume was intended for an English audience. "Song of the Lonely Bachelor" and "Nursery Story: Modern Version" might well have appeared in the sickness section, both enforcing the idea of fear and alienation. Though well-crafted poems, they illustrate too well those fashionably prevalent twins of the fifties. Implicit in both poems is a specific culture, but they conform largely to the internationalists' concept. Humanity itself is the only measure of action and belief, humanity separated from all specific cultural references.

Since the country section of the book follows some people away from Ireland, such good poems as "Rome, Anno Santo" and "Soliloquy on a Southern Strand" fit well. The sense of loss of all the people when separated indicates the poet's view of the time: live in Ireland or live in meaningless exile. "Murphy in Manchester" shows an Irish laborer in economic exile who is more moved by a potato in a vegetable stall than by monuments to England's great men. Home is gone, and he lives in a foreign land. But this theme, carried over from *Forms of Exile,* is only part of *Poisoned Lands.* The important new poems in this section present the country and its people with great attractiveness and, often concurrently, distrust. "Like Dolmens Round My Childhood, The Old People" gives five examples of Irish country life, one, "Wild Billy Harbison who married a Catholic servant girl," unmistakably Ulster. Like all in this poem, Wild Billy is the victim of creeds and old hatreds which destroy life and joy.

The young poet must exorcise them and does so in a

poem that without its final magical passage might be all too regionalist to communicate to as wide an audience as it does:

> Ancient Ireland, indeed! I was reared by her bedside,
> The rune and the chant, evil eye and averted head,
> Formorian fierceness of family and local feud.
> Gaunt figures of fear and friendliness,
> For years they trespassed on my dreams,
> Until once, in a standing circle of stones,
> I felt their shadows pass
> Into that dark permanence of ancient forms.

Though striving to be free of the old, Montague instead finds his poetry haunted by them. In "The Mummer Speaks," he resurrects a scene that occurred frequently in the past, but seldom in Montague's present: the Christmas mummers who roar into farmhouses and enact the defeat of Satan. Here a passing scene remains in the poet's mind to be transmuted into an understanding of art: "The faces like listening animals,/The stormlamp swinging to and fro/. . ." The poet relieves his audience of the dull slowness of life, and a sensitive young viewer sees that art, "That purging lament of bad Times," can capture and lead one to understandings beyond his own experiences.

Many of these early poems show Montague's desire to comprehend the origins of his culture, but his instinctual awareness of the importance of the past far outdistances his information. "Wild Sports of the West," for instance, investigates the class structure in nineteenth-century terms with the characters of landowner, bailiff, and peasant-poacher. Their roles are fixed for all time, but Montague does not here go into their ancient prototypes. When confronted with

monuments of the far past, though, he wrote poems
lean and rich with a blend of the colloquial and
rhetorical. "A Royal Visit" is about Tara, and the pun
of the title places English rule of Ireland into the
forepart of time, where it belongs. Even St. Patrick is a
newcomer to this place, "This provincial magnificence."
Before the coming of this now discredited saint, existed
the old life of wolf-skinned warriors, "fisty men, " the
chanting bards, incantating druids which Montague, like
many in centuries since, has felt in his own blood raging
with Christian reproach against the wild, smelly ways of
the pagan.

The struggle of epic remembrances with the closely
reasoned history of Judeo-Christian men frequently
causes dissonance in Montague's poetry. It is the theme
of "Old Mythologies," which may be the best poem in
this volume:

> And now, at last, all proud deeds done,
> Mouths dust-stopped, dark they embrace
> Suitably disposed, as urns, underground. . . .
> The valley cradles their archaic madness
> As once, on an impossibly epic morning,
> It upheld their savage stride:
> To bagpiped battle marching,
> Wolfhounds, lean as models,
> At their urgent heels.

Any reckoning made of the inheritance of Yeats must
value this poem highly for the unpretentiously melodic
long line, the clean and sparse diction, the exactness of
detail, the preservation of a spent view of life. Often in
consciously mythic poems, Montague will write with
such self-imposed limitations, but the contemporary
element that is found only in the simile "lean as
models" will dominate later.

Ireland has not been found appealing in the first part of *Poisoned Lands:* ruined lands inhabited by ruined people, the flotsam of a wrecked culture. Yet, as true in *Forms of Exile,* no other place offers artistic refuge. In "Stills" he sets an emblem of modern corruption, showing with photographic exactness "Four suave and public men, in braided uniforms." Men of this kind have set administrative patterns into action which make even the warrior obsolete: "Softly swords rust in warriors' hands. . . ." From them exudes nothing natural. Death and birth become the same, for both occur in "Charnel Houses":

> The dawn darkens on the rubble
> Dissolves among slack shadows
> Among infested carrion
> Among loathsome privacies.

In the poem "Poisoned Lands" country people censure a land owner for his practice of putting out poison meat to kill predatory animals: "Four good dogs dead in one night/ And a rooster, scaly legs in the air,/ Beak in the dust, a terrible sight!" So evil and unnatural does he seem, the country believe him to be the devil incarnate, which is substantiated by his appearance in the poem:

> Privileged, I met him on an evening walk,
> Inveigled him into casual weather talk,
> 'I don't like country people' he said, with a
>   grin.

No utilitarian purpose motivates this modern extermination, but instead a malignancy. The poems of illness show a corrupted modern world, and even Ireland stuck on the backshelf of Europe has been touched.

The book in its original structure would have conformed to the mythic pattern of sickness and rebirth. Even in Montague's printed version, though, the fertility rite appears. In the last section, the country mummer-poet finds more complex and sophisticated forms; for art itself becomes the king who can destroy the blight. "Cultural Center" from *Forms of Exile,* now entitled "Musée Imaginaire," becomes with its new setting and title a compendium of art past and present. The description of "Room III, " beginning with the Catalan crucifix no longer censures America's jumbled taste, but asserts art's healing grace: "A complete abstraction judges us,/ From its clean white wall." "Woodtown Manor, " the title derived from a country house lived in by Morris Graves, presents the painter's imagined animals as having religious power to heal man's illness.

Though Ireland is often the scene, as in the above poem, Montague has no intention of becoming a local bard. He will be neither plowboy gadfly nor self-determined remanent of the Literary Renaissance. In "Regionalism, Or Portrait Of The Artist As A Model Farmer," Montague announces his preference for "fierce anonymity" rather than the more clearly defined character of some: "Wild provincials/ Muttering into microphones/ Declare that art/ Springs only from the native part." Montague neither then nor now, however, rejected Ireland as a subject. In "The First Invasion Of Ireland" he makes a tentative inquiry into ancient Irish history. Developing a scene from *Leabhar Gabhála, The Book of Conquests,* he tells of three men and fifty-one women, refused admittance to Noah's ark, who land in Ireland. Here Montague ironically contrasts that occasion with the present condition of Ireland:

Division of damsels they did there,
The slender, the tender, the dimpled, the round,

It was the first just bargain in Ireland,
There was enough to go round.

Concerned with accuracy, Montague now considers changing the word *first* to *last.* Though clever in conception and nimble in diction, this poem is stilted, much more so than will be Montague's later revivifications of Ireland's ancient past.

4
Death of a Chieftain

The stories in *Death of a Chieftain* were written largely in the early 60s and suggest the use of detail in the narrative poems Montague will write later. Very few of his poems in the first two volumes specifically concerned Ulster in image or theme; but those few evoked the provincialism, so often harsh, of the North. The stories, with two exceptions, concern Ulster or its people. Implicit in all is the bitter and recalcitrant spirit which Ulster's writers generally find among their countrymen. The stories, unlike some of the poems, do not risk being limited by so distinctive a subject. Having chosen the novelle as the form of his longer stories, Montague draws a story line that is elaborate, encrusted, and wayward. He has room to give the background of the area, to present vignettes and reflections on human life in general. The structure of the whole volume—not simply a random collection of stories—gives Montague even more freedom to develop his subject. The first five are about childhood and youth, with a country setting. The last four occur away from the Northern countryside with adult characters.

The volume appropriately begins with the Church and the education of the young. However, "That Dark Accomplice" presents a type of character who reappears several times later: the clever, polished, even sophisticated man who attempts to control all through the exercise of reason and power. In this story, a priest seems to enforce discipline because he enjoys destroying joy and individuality. After having been booed by the student body, he chose to punish one dull boy for a slight infraction by having him read to everyone from *The Lives of the Saints.*

The priest through most of the story resembles Melville's Claggart, one opposed to any form of natural goodness and joy. As the boys continue their opposition, though, he raves at them and then weeps. Revealed is his own lack of joy in shepherding a flock. Only duty, formed into a rigid imperative by uncompromising law, has supported him through his human failure.

The bleak background of Irish religion becomes specifically northern in "The Cry." The boy, now a young man working for an English newspaper, returns to visit his family. The first night home, he is awakened by the sound of a man being beaten in the street. His father tells him that such occurs often and encourages the son to write an article about the religious and political oppression in Ulster. The article remains unfinished because Peter finds no cooperation, except from his once militant father. The police, Protestant, refuse to admit anything of consequence has occurred. The man who was beaten and his family do not want to risk reprisals. Finally the village idiot scrawls a note: *"Nosy*

Parker go home." The sentiment recalls Camus' "The Guest," a story in which one man's nonpolitical and nonracial concern for another isolates him from everyone.

Binding all the stories together is what once would have been called "the theme of alienation," usually complex. In "The Oklahoma Kid," for instance, the separation of the young boy from his birthplace in the United States and his momentary strangeness in town become so much the pattern of his life that he identifies with the dispossessed. Years later he talks to a man in an Oklahoma cafe:

> 'I'm a Cherokee from Tulsa,' he said, with what I took to be both fatalism and pride. 'What part of Oklahoma do you come from?'
> 'From Oklahoma City,' I said, involuntarily, 'County Tyrone,' and choked with a mixture of joy, shame and ridiculous conceit.

The autobiographical is not even disguised here, but of more importance is the wide significance of the character.

The theme and character reappear, pleasingly as well as expectedly, in "The Road Ahead," which tells of another homecoming. Another young man meets a childhood friend on a country road. As they talk, cars race each other along the new road ("'There's a queer change,' he said, indicating the road."). The mechanical world has touched and corrupted the whole countryside, including the spring, which has been given a concrete wall with an opening to emit the water. The old ways pass, as will the countryman with his belief in spells and magic. With the advance of technology through concrete ways and means, all belief not based on profit and reason will be challenged and perhaps fall.

Montague's concern is not always internationalist. In "The New Enamel Bucket" he shows an occurrence that can happen anywhere but is, in spite of that, Ulster's own. Two men after a fair are bilked and beaten by toughs in the locally notorious town of Moorhill:

> As the first blow struck him, sharply, in the back of the neck, below the ear, John Rooney turned, astonishment and shock lengthening his features. 'We're all friends here, men,' he said, with obscure conviction. The next blow caught him full on the mouth and he staggered backwards. Just as he was wondering what to say or do, all the grave-stones in the Protestant cemetery began to topple in on him, avengingly.

The religious reference continues as a major concern in Montague's Ulster writings. Just as much part of the character of these people, perhaps even a necessary part of their religious fervor, is the senseless and spontaneous violence. (Papa in "The Oklahoma Kid" is ready to hit people in the cinema because they object to his talking, for instance.)

Predictably, the locale of the stories moves to the South when Montague writes of an adult character. Not only was the same change made by Montague; but Dublin is, as it has been traditionally, the social and cultural center of the whole of Ireland. The story, "A Change of Management," marks the beginning of the last half of the volume. This story, along with "The Cry" and "Death of a Chieftain," stylistically contrasts with most of the other stories, those which develop a narrative smoothly and keep the reader conscious of all developments. Like a minuscule *Ulysses,* this story traces twenty-four hours in the life of John O'Shea and witnesses a change from the traditional bumbling Irish

administrator to the new, efficient, determined one who
has shaped (for good and ill) the modern world. Dr.
William Pearse Clohessy is calculating and convinced of
the patriotic service he renders in becoming the new
Irish administrator. No accident occurs in his life, as
indicated by his successful following of the life plan he
described when he was at the University, honors student
to first-class bureaucrat. O'Shea must choose between
the old, casual life of Dublin's past or accept Clohessy's
way, which will bring in a steel and glass world to
replace the accustomed Georgian structures.

Clohessy means more than a change in architecture,
obviously. The first monument to fall is Tadgh Cronin, a
stereotype of the hard-drinking Dublin man of letters
paid by the government for doing an inconspicuous
amount of work. On leaving his position, he
bombastically predicts a future of "Factories owned by
Germans, posh hotels catering to the grey flannel
brigade, computers instead of decent pen-pushers. . . ."
Cronin will more than likely die, but not because he
opposes the coming of a world of efficient sameness;
alcohol will in time destroy either his heart or his liver.
He will become another example of the Irishman
displaced by a changing world. That he is any worse off
than O'Shea, who will follow where he is led, is
doubtful. Both may well be part of a species endangered
by an increasingly inhuman world.

"A Change in Management," without attempting to
sway the reader, does nostalgically summon the old way
of Dublin life. But Montague does not pretend that the
new way will destroy an especially desirable life. "An
Occasion of Sin" shows Catholicism in Southern Ireland

as inculcating a life existing at extremes: mindless innocence or prurient suspicion. A young Frenchwoman, married to an Irishman, swims each day at a beach and tutors in French young men who are studying for the priesthood. She is warned by a kindly man on the beach that she is being gossiped about because of her contact with the clerical students. Shocked, she finds her husband's mind to be cloistered also, entirely within the Jansenist structure that has fashioned Irish Catholicism. He tells her that she is probably regarded as an occasion of sin. To her astonishment, only their marriage keeps him from considering her as do the others.

So many of the people in these stories are the unwitting objects of ancient meanness that the appearance of a guilty, though disturbed, man offers an informative contrast. Bernard Corunna Coote is a renegade Ulster Protestant, one who has abandoned the ways of his forefathers. Destruction of the enemy Catholics, and war in general, repulses him. His one obsessive drive is to prove that a unified Celtic race settled not only Europe but also the Americas. The legend of St. Brendan forms the basis for his suspicion, and the discovery of archeological remains in Panama that resemble some in Ireland sets his purpose: the discovery of a burial chamber identical to the ones in Ireland.

Montague has given himself opportunity to digress, in the fashion of novelle writers, to provide a variety of tangential information: racial lore of the Americas, archeological finds at Newgrange, the circumstances that produced the Orangemen. All of this is loosely tied to the story of Bernard. Though he is not understood by the group of outcasts he meets in the jungle, he is loved by them. They try to give form to his theory by having such a building as he searches for made by the Indians in his employ. On discovering the deception, he enters and collapses the walls of the sepulchre. Both Catholic and Protestant regiments parade in Coote's mind at the end, suggesting an end to old animosities. Coote, who is burdened with guilt for the crimes and offenses of his ancestors who dispossessed their neighbors, can function only in a make-believe world. So strongly does he want to right the wrongs, he devotes his life and death to the glory that was Celticdom, or at least should have been.

No censure is made of Coote because he pursues an irrational ideal; for increasingly in these early works, Montague questions the value of reason. In "A Ball of Fire," the last story in the book, an artist allows himself to be controlled by the instinctive and to be at the play of forces he cannot understand. (The story itself is structurally conventional.) Michael Gorman is a controlled and somewhat unambitious painter. After a few meetings with an enigmatic neighbor, whose quietness upsets Gorman, he becomes obsessed with the man. Inexplicably, after one meeting, Gorman begins a disturbing and, to him, incomprehensible painting. Only after the other man's death does he return to it. On the dark canvas, a line "ran right across the canvas until, completing and culminating the picture, it finished in a smothered explosion of colour, like a ball of fire." The strange little man resembles a ball of fire as he bustles down the street. Both he and the painting are conditions of existence that ˙Gorman does not comprehend. Whether or not the man, Daly, is happy or sad never becomes relevant; for his is energy unrestrained by convention. The nexus between Daly and Gorman is irrational and so, perhaps, can not be expressed as understandably as the guilt of Coote, the estrangement of the boy at the cinema.

In these short stories, Montague has gained experience with narrative form and the use of detail that will help him with the long narrative poems which form *The Rough Field.* But the stories merit discussion for themselves. Within such open and embellished structures, Montague has been able to take his readers into the private world of Ireland, especially Ulster. Even the confused violence of Ulster becomes somewhat better understood as we get to know Montague's lonely and defensive characters, who so seldom allow their minds to function outside inherited categories and prejudices.

5

A Chosen Light,
Home Again,
All Legendary Obstacles

A Chosen Light was long overdue when it appeared. However, in the meantime, Montague had written a volume of quite exceptional short stories. And, he had begun the examination of his place in the culture of Ireland (North and South) which later grows into the long poem called *The Rough Field.* Well settled in Paris when writing *A Chosen Light,* he looked at Ireland from the distance of the Irish writer in exile, with memory sharpened by frequent visits. Both the organization of the volume and the manner of its publication reflect Montague's multicultural concerns. The first section was published separately at the Dolmen Press in Dublin under the title *All Legendary Obstacles.* "The Country Fiddler," the second section, was published with poems from "The Cage" and two unpublished poems as *Home Again* by Queen's University of Belfast.

A Chosen Light, structured as it is, leads the reader to understand the magic of art and life in the final section,

"Beyond the Liss," by making him, in the first section, "All Legendary Obstacles," aware of dangers that can inhibit life. The passing answer of simple people is given in "The Country Fiddler," the second section; while "The Cage," the third, tells of the traps in our modern world. However, this sectional division seems intended to help the reader enter the distinctive world of an Irish poet become European. The same theme runs through all: the struggle of an Ulster Catholic to find cultural referents for his own affirmation of gentleness, love, and compassion. The society of Ulster has not in modern times been founded on order, roles, and dignity. The passing of the O'Neills signaled the beginning of a new harsh, violent, petty life.

A Chosen Light does not deal directly with political problems, but the poet as persona of the country reveals its problems. Montague explores the harsh meanness and violence that can be readily associated with any part of the world that has lost or not achieved an ordered structure. "Country Matters" tells of a pretty young girl pursued by men until "no one 'decent'/ Or 'self-respecting' would touch her." She probably is found everywhere; but in rural areas she is seen so often as to be a type: brief careless joy leading to a dull, sad life. Though life is often loose in the country, morality is strict, love a luxury, and Montague's conclusion to the poem an apt summary:

> For lack of courage
> Often equals lack of a language
> And the world of love is
> Hardest to say.

Though many know the experience, few have made it part of their art.

Montague makes the destruction of a trivial person emblematic of a general state of pain and loss. He knows the lack of language, the loss of speech that creates the easy world of clichés in which none needs think or struggle. In "Obsession" he tells of a recurring memory that stuns him and strikes him inarticulate; and ordeal and trauma are often subjects in this volume, especially in the first section. "That Room" exemplifies a frequent technique. The poet tells that within a room two people found an understanding which changed their lives. Specific causes are omitted, for Montague here charts a pattern and does not describe an event. "A Private Reason" shows a man and woman lost in private thought. The refrain, which recalls the unknown relationship between Dean Swift and Vanessa, suggests problems of duplicity and doubt between the two people: "as we/ Walked out by Merval."

The poems describe the difficulties of a person growing from a childishly simple society into an adult one. "Return," the title being a frequent subject for Montague, summarizes the duality:

> Seeing your former
> self saunter up the garden path
> afterwards, would you flinch,
> acknowledging
> that sensuality,
> that innocence?

Quite likely, one can see the problems and peculiarities of another culture better than those of his own. However, outside Ireland flesh and joy do not seem to cause such intense or long-lasting torment.

That Montague treats his and others' fleshly difficulties without comedy differentiates him from

most of his predecessors and many of his
contemporaries. As Vivian Mercier has shown in *The
Irish Comic Tradition,* sex and death both arouse such
fear and awe in the Irish that they have traditionally
been the subjects of comedy. Even though Montague's
treatment of sex avoids the usual humor, the fear is
frequently there. "The Trout," for instance, is a thinly
described description of masturbation and was called "a
love poem" by Montague on the cover of a record
album, *The Northern Muse:*

> The two palms crossed in a cage
> Under the lightly pulsing gills.
> Then (entering my own enlarged
> Shape, which rode on the water)
> I gripped. To this day I can
> Taste his terror on my hands.

Another reason for the Irishman's typical reaction to
the sexual may well be his view of women. Robert
Graves in *The White Goddess* has, with the agreement of
many, established matriarchy as the structure of ancient
Celtic society. Believing in racial memory, as he does,
Montague's presentation of the woman as muse and
goddess may well be a conscious recreation of ancient
mythic patterns. In "The Gruagach" Montague tells of
the way a mountain recalls to the minds of locals the
ancient Scotish Gaelic goddess, "the brute-thighed
giantess. . . ." Even more commonplace events elicit a
similar response from Montague, as, for instance, in
"Virgo Hibernica" in which trudging "docile" by a
woman's flank he feels "the gravitational pull/ of love."
Increasingly, Montague's lyrics attempt to express the
ritual giving significance and form to the details of
experience. To enter into that ritual is often to accept a

nonrational (perhaps mystical) union of self and mythic order and identity.

The terror-evoking power of even young women in Montague's poems becomes the essential identity of old women. They often appear as hags used by the neighborhood to frighten children into behaving. Actually, though, they only frighten because their extreme old age separates them from the present. They touch the past in their remembered experiences. Because they provide an entry to a more stable time for Montague, they often resemble the Sybil. In "The Answer" a chance meeting with an old woman informs Montague of the old, gracious way of life that has almost past:

> While friendly,
> unafraid, the woman turned her face
> like a wrinkled windfall, to proffer
> the ritual greetings:
> > *Dia dhuit/*
> *Dia agus Muire dhuit/*
> > *Dia agus Muire*
> *agus Padraig dhuit*
> > Invocation of powers
> to cleanse the mind.

This old woman is frightening or curious only in a Christian context. She is residue from a time before the Christian word. In "The Centenarian," television cameras record an old woman's hundredth birthday. Not only age but experience separate her from the present. She, her beliefs, her God are out of place in the present.

She is not only an Irish type, but occurs in any country. Montague met her, again, selling newspapers in Paris:

And when I asked the woman at the kiosk
'Il y a quelque chose de nouveau?
She said: 'C'est tout dans le journal.'
She probably said that before the *Blitzkrieg.*

These old women removed from easy identification with the present seem to lead Montague to find a correspondence between himself and them. By his vocation and by his ready sympathy for the misplaced, the outsiders, he appears ill at ease in the order of the modern European world. He does, however, understand it and reflect in his poems some of its natural beauty as well as its mechanical regularity.

A considerable part of Montague's concern in this volume is with his adjusting to living in Paris. In the poem, "A Chosen Light," he finds a moment of peace where he lives, "In that stillness-soft but luminously exact,/ A chosen light. . . ." And in the same poem, Samuel Beckett appears in a quite different, though equally sure, quiet light: "He plots an icy human mathematics—/ Proving what content sighs when all/ Is lost, what wit flares from nothingness. . . ." Surrounding these two is the light of an order Montague does not accept, and which he suggests is also strange to Beckett. The ordered affluent world of the French finds an emblem of itself for Montague in the light of a radiometer, "ceaselessly/ Elaborating its signals/ Not of help, but of neutral energy." Since such life has existed in Europe for centuries, one may wonder a bit about Montague's sardonic censure of it.

Though Montague finds that his life and his beliefs allow him to share the experience of a wide variety of people, there continues to be a kernel of identity in him that is forever Ulster. In "Waiting," life in Paris takes him back to wartime Ulster with its German prisoners, its air-raid alerts, and the bombing of Belfast, "the grit/ Of different experience, of shared terror/ No swift neutral sympathy can allay," when the fire engines came from the South to help put out fires in bombed Belfast. Hopefully accepting any sign of a united Ireland, Montague celebrates an act of human kindness.

Montague's accustomed way of presenting Ireland is through the experience of his acquaintances or family. In "The Road's End," another poem about returning to his childhood home, he describes the decline in population:"Like Shards/ Of a lost culture, the slopes/ Are strewn with cabins, emptied." Especially in writing about country people, Montague makes heavy use of place names and family names: the Blind Nialls, Big Ellen, Jamie MacCrystal. The simple, leisurely people of the country become expendable in the efficiency of the modern world, as Montague suggests in "The Hen House" and in "Hill Field."

Perhaps because he writes mostly about country people, Montague generally writes of the Irish as bitter, flawed, or failing. Two family poems illustrate the theme. In "The Cage," he describes his father, an Irish exile in New York, as "the least happy/ man I have known." In part, exile itself cost him happiness; but the poem also stresses that Irish narrowness encloses minds as tightly in exile as at home. The Ulster tendency to hold its own tightly, even unto death, is the theme of "Family Conference." For an old woman, life is locked into the past:

Today grandchildren
Call, but what has she to say
To the buoyant living, who may
Raise family secrets with the dead?

In "Witness," a dying old man torments his children by threatening to disinherit them.

The continuance of past ways, whether they help or hinder people, must be expected in a culture as conservative as that of Ireland. For over seven centuries, the mere Irish have held to an idea of self that has ceased to be practicable and perhaps never did exist in the way it is "remembered." P. S. O'Hegarty in *Ireland Under the Union* defined this idea of self: "But they had, through their National language, their memory. . . , memory of every binding thing that is in a folk memory, and they had their indomitable tenacity."

Often in Montague's poetry the present has been rejected, but not simply because it is different. He has opposed what limits the human being to dullness, what denies joy. In *A Chosen Light,* Montague indicates two ways of avoiding the caged life Ireland so often offers. In "The Siege of Mullingar," young people reject the life style effected in Ireland by Victorian England and Jansenist-laced Catholicism: "Bottles in/ Hand, they rowed out a song:/ *Puritan Ireland's dead and gone,/ A myth of O'Connor and O'Faolain."*/ Montague's celebration of a new, though harsh, strain in Irish culture isolates one part of contemporary life. He finds, however, the most satisfying freedom from past inhibitions in the experience of the artist. "Beginnings" describes what he sees as the source of cultural and individual life: "Beginnings of a language,/ first sign to escape from darkness,/ scrawl on a cave wall. . . ." Repeatedly in this volume, Montague designates art as capable of bringing life. Implicit always is a social order which grants to the artist a persona he must struggle to fit. Art and order exist together and ideally strive to create personal happiness and social stability. *Ideally* must be stressed. For the individual's struggle with a persona never ends, and dissonance is eternal.

In "Beyond the Liss" Montague presents an analogy of the poet through "Sean the hunchback," who steps into the world of faery. Believing that all poets have quirks, deformities, which separate them from the rest of the population, Montague shows the difficulty of such a person. Though capable of transporting himself beyond commonness, beyond deformity, into the magic world of beauty, he cannot continue in such happiness. Montague's similarity to the confessional poets of contemporary America is evident here. But unlike them, he chooses to employ a persona rather than his own bare psyche.

The poems in *A Chosen Light* vacillate between inquiries into personal and social difficulties and unpleasantnesses and celebrations of joy when the poet has found a pleasing persona. The last poem, "The True Song," sums up Montague's attempt to assume the persona. For emblems of beauty, death, and victimage, he has a swan, a lady, and "a stricken one":

> For somewhere in all this
> Stands the true self, seeking
> To speak, who is at once
> Swan
>   lady
>   stricken one.

Here all is myth and metaphor. And undoubtedly, Montague intends many of his specifically Irish poems, such as "The Siege of Mullingar," to exist in the same metaphoric state. However, that achievement must ultimately be judged by history.

Yeats was able to use place names, particular events, and specific individuals mythically for at least two reasons: he was a conscientious systematizer, and he drew his attitudes and personae from an established literary tradition. But for the contemporary poet, such as Montague, the personal, even the individual trauma, is frequently the subject. The thing is important in itself, not because of metaphoric association. The personal involvement of the poet in the poem, without benefit of persona, and his desire to achieve a persona demand that the critic distinguish between the two and understand the reason for both.

Essentially, today's poet cannot step comfortably into the world of legend as he would like it to be. Modern scholarship has made the past all too immediate for him. And those ancient times seem more like the flawed present than the ideal lands poets have always wanted them to be. Kinsella's translation of the *Tain,* for instance, shows heroic Ulster to have much in common with strife-ridden Londonderry. Montague in his attention to detail in describing scenes and people attempts to present the ritual underlying them. At times, the details are so specific that one can simply say, that is the thing itself. Usually, this occurs when he writes about Ireland rather than about France. Whether because the subject is limiting in itself or readers are often limited, one often steps into specifically Irish poems with difficulty. However, an internationalist poet such as Montague must consider the culture of present-day Ireland as valid a subject as that of any other country.

6
Tides

Tides, like Montague's earlier verse, is essentially concerned with describing the rituals giving form to the details of life. However, the individual poems within the structure of the whole volume have a greater psychic fury than the earlier. This is not to say that they are all among the best poems Montague has written. Many are, but the volume itself gives added strength to individual poems because it is so tightly unified by concern with death and destruction. Perhaps the deaths of father and grandmother and his meeting with the muse as Medusa forced this quite constant concern in Montague's writing into obsession. The poetry is not morbid, for all its dwelling on the subject, because Montague tries to give "an answer to death." Curiously, the structure of the volume resembles that of the traditional elegy.

"Premonition," which opens the volume, presents a by-now-obsessive image in Montague's poetry: the nightmarish carving up of a woman's body. As in "Obsession," which began *A Chosen Light,* one infers that dreamer and tormentor are the same. But here the ending gives added concern:

> On the butcher's block
> Of the operating theatre
> You open your eyes.
> Far away, I fall back
> Towards sleep, the Liffey
> Begins to rise, and knock
> Against the quay walls.

The image of pain is part of a pattern in which death and life, pain and joy, rise and fall as necessarily as the tides. The pattern continues in all of life and may be traced in the details even of lovers' quarrels. "Summer Storm" tells of such anger and its exorcism in a garish scene as two people squash mosquitoes on each other. Both become dominated by the rising and falling pattern manifest in the woman's body. Identification of sea and woman's body occurs frequently in mythic literature and here prepares for the last section of the book, "Sea Changes," in which Montague presents the patterns without obvious recourse to the human. "King & Queen" in this part of *Tides* and later "To Cease" show his extension of the pattern of change from human to non-human. Like "The Gruagach" in *A Chosen Light* these poems present monolithic earth forms which evoke awe because they have the fixity of fundamental forms of creation.

"The Wild Dog Rose" and "The Hag of Beare" are the two most likely in the whole book to be complete in themselves. Both were, by the way, published separately. Taken as companion poems, they show how the sexual experiences of two totally different women transform Christian figures into beauty and love, in contrast with the frequent austerity and antagonism of

Christianity in Northern Ireland. Again, Montague's concern is with transformations in people who are touched or controlled by patterns which give shape to all creation.

"The Wild Dog Rose" begins with a description now familiar in Montague's writing: "that terrible figure who haunted my childhood. . . ." The old women of "The Answer" and of "Waiting" occur again here. And like them she is a crone, so old she belongs to another time, existing now as a reminder of the past. For many, she seems a wicked creature, a hag akin to Kali the goddess of death. Her age and ugliness remove her from general experience, but these it seems most draw Montague to her. He writes, "Memories have wrought reconciliation/ between us. . . ." Her deformity brings them closer, "lovers almost," suggesting Montague's obsessive concern with the artist's own deformity. This separates him from active people, those at ease in the company of strangers. But in the company of people he does not feel the need to deceive, Montague is a different creature. Then the deformity becomes his entry into another's pain.

The old woman's loneliness, terrifying in itself, becomes accentuated after a drunk attempts to rape her. Through his friendship with her, however, Montague understands that her loneliness and later her abuse have led her to create beauty. During the attack she prayed to the Virgin Mary, whom she credits with saving her. Living alone in the country, the old woman creates her own objects of worship from her surroundings. "Each bruised and heart-shaped petal" of the wild dog rose reminds her of the Virgin Mary and "all she suffered."

The virgin becomes in this creation beautiful, human, and understanding. And the old woman's ugliness is only the sign of her separation from the people around her, ones quite likely to regard her as evil and the Virgin as a battlecry. Both are the rose whose beauty comes from suffering in life and from a love that becomes faith.

"The Hag of Beare," a version rather than a translation, has a quite different woman as narrator. But like the one in "The Wild Dog Rose," her life shows the large pattern of joy, loss, and beauty. She too creates from love that has become belief. But this old woman knew and loved the world. She, an aging courtesan, mottled in skin, one eye gone, and infirm in all ways, remembers the homage she was once paid, when she lived by her skills, developed into arts. Now she finds neither the way nor the will to practice them; mean and petty days have come, and she has no hope either of their return or the return of her youth.

The hag, at whatever time in her life, made a transformation as important as aging when she came to Christ. But even in this quite schematized ritual, she both viewed and accepted him in her own terms:

Well might the Son of Mary
Take their place under my roof-tree
For (if) I lack other hospitality
I never say 'No' to anybody—

However, in presenting Christ as a desirable man, she has created a companion religious figure to the human Mary in the preceeding poem. The pairing of these two in an other than mother-son relationship would not be out of the ordinary in many religions based on the fertility cycle, as Frazer repeatedly illustrated in *The Golden Bough.*

Clearly, Montague presents Christianity within the framework of Celtic belief. In "The Wild Dog Rose," identification of the cailleach is with an ancient goddess of death. "The Hag of Beare," as Montague explains in his comment in *Ireland of the Welcomes* (Jan.-Feb. 1969), was a member of a female order of poets in Celtic times. Though Montague is concerned to show "the struggle between paganism and Christianity, between worldly pleasure and the doctrine of salvation through repentance," as important to him is the contemporary significance of the poem. In part of *The Rough Field,* Montague will return to the theme of the psychological struggle between Christian and pagan identity in a woman to arrive at the same conclusion as in these two poems. His poetry is centered on celebration of the muse, the ancient goddess who occurs in three phases: mother, lover, destroyer. Though he does not deny the importance of Christianity, he stresses the physical love and the celebration of the ritual of the year which it should share with those religions it most resembles.

After having expressed the appeal and continued force of mythic identity and patterns in the first section, Montague then explains the dangers. The tides before were at the ebb, bringing memories of past days; they are now the tides that wreck, that bring terror and destruction. Describing a seafront resort in "North Sea," Montague fantasizes in terms of one of his recurring obsessions: "the almost forgotten monster/ of unhappiness...clank[s] ashore/ (an old horror movie come true)." When he chooses, as in "The Oklahoma Kid," Montague handles even the mechanical parts of contemporary culture with humor and conviction. Usually, though, he attacks nonhuman forces as destructive and antithetical to his often bucolic muse. In this poem he successfully combines the two approaches by drawing an image from the late movies, to which he is addicted.

The tinge of humor does not, however, mask the horror, and his fascination with it, in the other poems of this section. In "The Pale Light," the muse appears as a sexual experience that is awry. Her genitals have been moved to her head, and the danger of such sexual knowledge appears in hissing snakes. Whatever the actual form of the experience, its effect is to introduce death into the poet's life: "heavily she glides towards me/Rehearsing the letters of my name. . . ." The pun in "Rehearsing" stresses the destruction, but in the pale light of morning he can see his intercourse with Medusa as the sign of "death being born." In a sensual understanding so powerful that all life seems stolen from death, man matches the creative experience of the artist, who himself steals time from death. To love the muse is to envision a world beyond sensuality and to know how brief a container of that experience the body is.

Emphasis in this section continues to be on pain, the exonerating quality of it generally more obliquely stated than in "Pale Light." Two prose passages are especially difficult, being as they are unexplained images of suffering. "Coming Events" describes a man being flayed alive and ends with:

> The whole scene may be intended as an allegory of human
> suffering but what the line of perspective leads us to admire
> is the brown calfskin of the principal executioner's boots.

In "The Huntsman's Apology," another prose piece, a
killer justifies his acts by contrasting them with those of
the scavenger, who preys on weak and wounded
animals. Though the kill gives him belief in his power,
the scavenger is actually like one who woos the muse
with his own unhappiness rather than the joy of life,
death and birth. The power of the cycle is so great and
dominating that one must either celebrate it or
maliciously resist the flow by structuring the natural
into unnatural forms. Montague writes of both
possibilities.

After the blackness of "The Pale Light," the next
section of *Tides* opens into the bright, clearness of day.
In another poem based on a ninth-century Irish original,
Montague tells of the fertility king and his muse, or
great goddess, who "gave him black fruit from thorns/&
the full of his arms /of strawberries, where they lay."
June 29, or St. John's Day, does not singly proclaim a
life of joy, and neither does Montague's poem. In both,
a ritual brings life and death to the king, simulating the
decline of summer and anticipating its return.

In the rituals cited by Frazer, homeopathic magic is
employed; and perhaps Montague intends the same in
poems describing the rituals by which passion is
aroused and satisfied. "The Same Gesture," for
instance, erects a metaphoric equation between the
shifting of gears in a car and the ones which "eased your
snowbound/ heart and flesh." (Though the figure seems
somewhat strained to me, I do know people who derive

erotic stimulation from the automobile.) More important in this poem is Montague's separating the magical experience of two lovers from their usual passage through the day. Implicit here is a censure of the contemporary work-a-day world, which continues in "Life Class," the titular poem of this section. Here the poet watches a woman modeling nude for a drawing class and muses about the various roles she must play. She is, of course, an anatomical problem for the class. Montague's mind, probably like that of the others, gives values of love and passion to the bare body. These thoughts lead him, as one expects of the Irish, to consider her as did the "desert fathers." For them she would be the very image of destruction: "breasts, dangling/ tresses to drag man/ down to hell's gaping/ vaginal mouth." The role of destroyer has frequent associations in myth, but that ugliness is implicit in all women more properly belongs to the Christian tradition, as Montague has indicated. Continued censure of wrong ways of viewing the woman, as an object, appears in the way fashion designers would mould her to fit their conception, resulting in "a uniformity/ of robot bliss."

In actuality, the woman-mother-wife-whatever exists in terms not to be captured by the "army of pencils" in the hands of the students, by the words of the poet, the conception of the designer. She may encompass all, but none may completely encompass her just as life itself always exceeds our every conceptualization. This theme is reiterated in "Earthbound." Despite the moon landings, "the pale-faced/ imperious virgin/ who rules our best/ dreams still strides/ the night. . . ." The section ends with the returning sound of *tides,* stressing the return of life. Expectedly, though, danger remains part of the relationship between poet and muse, or even part of the erotic life. For the muse may assume forms out of the ordinary.

Before opening the pattern of the tides to its widest, Montague narrows to reveal a personal and immediate obstacle (though he might prefer the vaguer term of condition): the past and present of Northern Ireland as they affect his life. Here the first poem gives title to the section, and "The Northern Gate" sets the tone as Montague recalls the hoot of an owl, "clearing his throat/ somewhere behind me," only to be drowned out by "a sigh of airbrakes/ from a morning lorry." In the conversational tone of the internationalists, Montague uses a traditional death bird, the owl, to announce the death of wilderness and nature as the mechanical world expands control. Though the tone of this section is consistently deathly, there is complexity in the variety of transformations possible. In "To Cease" Montague considers erratic humanity becoming a natural monolithic monument. Though he may envision such a state, Montague himself is not close to entering it. He has not moved completely into a new order, in part because the world around him has not and in part because he has not completely freed himself from old limitations.

In two elegiac poems, he writes of that past. "Last Journey" considers the death of his father, who had bred his son to long for County Tyrone. But the son has come and gone, and now the father and his conception of the land pass. The death of the father does not completely sever Montague from the past. As much as humanly possible, the death of his grandmother, who raised him, and is described in "Omagh Hospital," does. The old woman, delirious and dying, asks her grandson to take her home. He remembers her house, "shaken by traffic/ until a fault runs/ from roof to base." The "fault," if one remembers Montague's poem with the same words for title, achieves metaphoric value for him. Like the land, he too is flawed, broken by weakness and strength as well. He can bury emblems of the past, but must force his mind away from contemporary entanglements to break the domination of that past. However, he does not seem willing to abandon his country and his time during the great turmoil of Ulster.

The new machine age, contemporary ethics, and political approaches tear Ireland, especially the North, into hostile camps. Even within one man, rival beings war, calling for miraculous and ameliorative transformations. Only two offer themselves, and one is found by his grandmother on her hospital bed as she drifts "towards nothingness." The alternative to death, currently so popular in Northern Ireland, is a dissimilation of warring spirits under peace, currently so unpopular in Northern Ireland. In "What a View," which echoes the ending of *The Bread God,* Montague takes for his persona the sea gull, that makes no distinctions based on name, race, religion. Last seen, the seagull has lightened his load for flight on the British flag and is heading out to sea. Though consistent with Montague's portrayal of the bird as unable to differentiate between people in political terms, by choosing to close with a defecation, he has given a parting shot that cannot be misunderstood. The fault remains, no matter who created it.

The seagull's setting out to sea, however, introduces the last section of the volume, *Sea Changes*. Here the ocean and its inhabitants, including man, find themselves controlled by a complex, unifying pattern.

The subtitle to this section, "A Sequence of Poems for Engravings by William Hayter," stresses Montague's concern with a general, even abstract pattern, as William Hayter's etching on the front of *Tides* shows. Though more objectively realistic than some of Hayter's, the etching represents his concern with rhythmic, wavelike forms.

The merging of female form into waves, though, does not dominate "Sea Changes." In fact, after the initial poem, only one specifically sexual distinction is drawn. In "Boats," Montague continues his search for unions between Christian and pagan belief. "Remous" stresses another of Montague's themes in this volume: the ecstatic and cataclysmic possibilities of sexual love. He enters this discussion of a dangerous point in the sea, the whirlpool, with an obvious but effective pun:

> The seamen, sea-
> gulls sense a change,
> a shift in the wind
> flick of raindrops
> on feather or face;
> an unusual calm. . . .

The poem develops, obliquely, Montague's concern with the magic of sexuality.

Somewhat distracting, because of frequent occurrence, is Montague's stressing of the cataclysmic. In "Lame de Fond," perhaps the strongest poem in this last section, he reiterates a foreboding theme: relentless, inevitable power. Earlier in the poem was a seemingly more hopeful view: "Die or devour! But/ Everything dies into birth." Describing the life of sea creatures, Montague presents again the cyclic order in which death but prepares for life, in which the past lies inert, though nutritive, under the present. However, one wonders if the most powerful wave of all moving silently across the bottom of the ocean can not throw all before it into havoc. Would it follow ancient patterns and obliterate a life not in accord with it? destroy all? The same problem comes to mind when I read Montague's poem *A New Siege* in *The Rough Field.* Is Ulster, and Ireland in general, captured in an ancient destructiveness? Will there be enough to build on? An optimist, like Toynbee, would say, "World War III will not destroy all life." Perhaps only the old, the hags for instance, can face mindless destruction so calmly.

Montague makes clear in this book, as he has before, that his concern is with historical as well as psychological and physical patterns. In "Wine Dark Sea" he consciously instructs in a broad perspective. The sea is the "sea of history/ on which we all turn/ turn and thresh/ and disappear." Even here, in a poem that seems so studiedly calm, anxiety enters minds entangled with history in a prediction of nothingness. Yeats, for instance, regarded man's release from the cycle of death and rebirth as the ultimate good. Perhaps in his seventies Montague will too, but now such release only seems an end to entanglements that may lead to knowledge but not to single happiness. Ambivalence is stressed repeatedly. In "Filet" the nets dropped over boats become symbolic of purpose which makes life possible and also that which ensnares instincts in "a tourniquet of death."

7

The Rough Field

Though Montague's concern with politics has been constant throughout his writing, his contemporaries generally regard him as a writer of love lyrics, probably because Montague's political concern has been oblique, an implicit examination of political and cultural conditions as they shape friends and family. Understandably, then, many people reacted with surprise and irritation as *The Rough Field* began to appear in pointedly political parts. The general approach in this long poem is one anticipated by Montague's other poetry. With the exception of *A New Siege*, which even the Taoiseach—Ireland's Premier—has commented on, the poems in *The Rough Field* examine the particular disintegration of Ulster's culture through the example of people close to the poet.

By the time *The Rough Field* is into print as a complete volume, all sections of it will have appeared in some form before except for two. This examination of Ulster by a poet after many years of exile reasonably begins with a version of *Home Again*, after which *The*

Leaping Fire concentrates specifically on his family.
Both of these are discussed in earlier chapters. In *The
Bread God,* which must be considered one of the
strongest sections of the whole long poem, family and
the culture of the North are openly related to one
another. Also in this section, Montague develops a form
of sufficient complexity to present the multilevels of
reality which constitute the religious and political
history of the North. The poem is presented as a
"lecture with illustrations in verse" which is transmitted
by radio and frequently interrupted by "pirate
stations." These surreptitious stations attempt to drown
out Montague's portrayal of Catholic life in the North
with Protestant war cries, such as " *'Cromwell went to
Ireland/ TO STOP/ The Catholics murdering
Protestants!'* " Here history is reversed.

The poem begins with a quotation from Carleton,
who describes a Roman Catholic Christmas service.
Thousands walk in a torchlight parade that must have
caused some unease among the Protestants of that area.
That uneasiness continues into the present, as indicated
by the war cries, even though the religious fervor is not
now what Carleton describes. Montague quotes a letter
from a Jesuit uncle: "I became a priest because we were
the most respectable family in the parish but what I
really wanted to do was join the army: so you see how
your uncle became a Jesuit!" A typical member of the
Church who arrives late is as casual as the priest, for
"On St. Joseph's/ Outstretched arm, he hangs his
cap. . . ." Alternating between Protestant attacks and
portrayals of people simply practicing a faith,
Montague's poem describes typical Sunday activities:

mass with Communion, a political speech to the docile
members, anticipations of football.

The violence of Penal Times is only suggested in
"Penal Rock/ Altamuskin," as Montague recalls a
country grotto that served as a place of worship for
Catholics denied their churches. He visits this place that
once was a shelter for his family, now all dispersed, and
imagines them at services:"long suffering as beasts,/But
parched for that surviving sign of grace. . . ."Omitted is
any direct reference to militancy among Catholics
today; but this poem was published in 1968, before the
violence in the North had become a way of life.

Montague's narrative mode allows him the freedom
to elaborate, to vary technique. And so just before the
ending of the poem, he returns to his uncle's letter:
"Your father, I know, was very bitter about having to
leave but when I visited home before leaving for the
Australian mission, I found our protestant neighbors
friendly, and yet we had lost any position we had in the
neighborhood." Following this colloquial statement
about his father's political exile, Montague
unexpectedly shifts to verse influenced by French
Surrealists and delivers "An Ulster Prophecy":

> I saw the Pope carding tow on Friday
> A blind parson sewing a Patchwork quilt/
> Three bishops cutting rushes with their croziers/
> Roaring Meg firing Rosary beads for cannonballs/
> Corks in boats afloat on the summit of the Sperrins/
> A mill and a forge on the back of a cuckoo/
> The fox sitting conceitedly at a window chewing tobacco/
> And a moorhen in flight
> > surveying   a United Ireland.

In this dissolving of paradoxes, Montague suggests the

end of strife in Northern Ireland over issues he regards as antithetical to the real purpose of Christianity and religion in general. Perhaps, as Montague said to me, the ancient celebration of the year will come to provide a common understanding leading to unity.

In the next three sections of *The Rough Field,* Montague will add two that have not yet been published: *The Severed Head,* which concerns the change from Irish to English as the language of Ireland, and *A Good Night,* which presents a boisterous night in a pub that turns harsh as the men get drunk. Between these is *The Fault,* which expands and elaborates the poem by the same title. In all three, Montague investigates a culture cut off from its source: the ancient Celtic language and culture. And each presents a people grown brutal and purposeless after the linguicide.

But the condition of Northern Ireland today cannot be simply described as the result of centuries of conflict with England. In *Hymn to the New Omagh Road,* Montague shows the destruction of the land with its attendant cultural associations, as modern industrial progress justifies its power by exercising it. Montague develops a form to present contemporary practices and aberrations and at the same time to recall a simpler and less-troubled past. Mixing contemporary and earlier images, Montague begins with a description of the destruction that is taking place:

> As the bull-dozer bites into the tree-ringed
>   hill fort
> Its grapnel jaws lift the mouse, the flower,
> With equal attention, and the plaited twigs
> And clay of the bird's nest, shaken by the traffic,
> Fall from a crevice under the bridge. . . .

Since progress and profit today remove all blame for any action, Montague gave his poem appropriate form when he made the first long section a balance sheet. Under "Loss" occur items—"primrose and dogrose"— one would hope, but not expect, a builder to value. The ironic "unlawful/ assembly of thistles" indicates the tone of the whole section, and is carried over as well into "Gain." Here Montague itemizes the small economic advance, an increase of ten miles per hour of average speed, which sometimes sends the driver straight into Garvaghey Graveyard.

Relating his family's history to the subject of the poem, he fantasizes about his dead grandfather, watching the cars speed past the graveyard. The contrast of the frantic and unreflective present with a past in which people lived more leisurely continues in the next section of the poem, "Glencull Waterside." Montague's description of the destruction wrought by "the crustacean jaws of the excavator" is contrasted with verses written by an earlier poet about this same glen: "On a lovely evening in spring (in nature's early pride)." By the end of the section, Montague has completed the contrast. All that remains of the glen as it had been is the poetry written about it.

Also rare is to find a poet concerned with the destruction of man himself by the scarcely challenged movement of the modern world into an impersonal and mass-produced artifact. In "Envoi: The Search for Beauty" Montague presents a small emblem of the modern world that, unfortunately, has very wide relevance: in front of a tract house, a concrete swan occupies a space meant for a tree. The variety of voices, and personae, assumed in this section of *The Rough Field*

suggests one of Montague's most distinctive character-
istics as a writer: his ability to adapt to another
person's manner with conviction. Though not a drama-
tist, he nevertheless presents a variety of characters in a
context which implies the tension and suspense of
drama.

In *Hymn to the New Omagh Road* the structure is
one familiar to readers of modern poetry; sections of
the poem are presented with immediacy but without
stated overall structure. The reader must be involved
sufficiently to relate the parts to each other and so
become the total structure himself. This has been the
intent of such long poems in this century as Eliot's *The
Waste Land,* Yeats's *The Tower,* and Dennis Devlin's
The Heavenly Foreigner; and so should not confuse a
reader of Montague. However, his use of personae
seldom has the ironic or aesthetic removal of Eliot or
Yeats; thus the character often becomes an empathetic
extension of Montague's own personality or bias. In the
last section of *The Rough Field, The Wild Dog Rose,*
this approach to poetry becomes his purpose. The poem
begins as a discussion of an old woman, develops
through her humanity, and ends with her identification
with the Virgin Mary and Montague's empathetic
celebration of humanity that must suffer.

Two sections appear before the final one, *The Wild
Dog Rose: Patriotic Suite* and *A New Siege.* Both of
these depict the effects of the 1916 Uprising in
contemporary Ireland, the first in the South and the
second in the North. Montague describes the theme of
Patriotic Suite as "Decay in the South;" but the poem
itself presents a somewhat more hopeful view of life in

the Republic. The poem begins by merging the ancient battle music of the Celts with a sound from nature, "the wail of tin/ whistle" and the "lost cry/ of the yellow bittern." So begun, the poem establishes an innate, racial quality of resistance in the Irish.

Poems II and III describe the absence of spirit in art following the Revolution: "The mythic lyre shrunk to country size." Though this poem is entitled "Traits and Stories," alluding to Carleton's stories about the North, the difficulty of post-Yeatsian Irish poets is accurately described. After the fervor and grandiose action of the Irish Literary Renaissance, poetry and life in the South often seemed trivial.

Obviously, much of *Patriotic Suite* must deal with the leaders and events of the 1916 Uprising. In "Revolution" Montague makes clear where his own sympathies lie:

> The bread queue, the messianic
> Agitator of legend
> Arriving on the train—
> Christ and socialism—
> Wheatfield and factory
> Vivid in the sun:
> Connolly's dream, if any one.

Connolly's socialist ideal appeals to Montague because, if put into practice, it might have kept the state from the boring sameness and bureaucratic structures of middle-class life—"the antlike activity of cars"—that Montague shows in "Enterprise." In the case of the hill tribes described in "Tribal Dance," the warriors are discarded by the population after the battles are over. The impersonal description of death and disaster of those who have become useless, even detrimental to the quiet business of peace, marks the failure of the revolutionary spirit to continue after the revolution.

In part this failure occurred because of the importance of the Anglo-Irish in fashioning the Revolution. Much of the cultural, and political, foundation of modern Ireland was provided by the non-Catholic, non-Irish, and non-proletarian part of its population. Section seven of *Patriotic Suite* assesses the value of the Anglo-Irish tradition to contemporary Ireland. Rather unfortunately, Montague concerns his comment only with the literary world, thus limiting scope. Also, his concern is further limited to Yeats and Lady Gregory. In "Abbey Theatre 1951" he presents Yeats's theatrical venture as moribund:

> In this gutted building, a young man might stand,
> Watching a firehose play, like a soothing hand.
> It has earned little of his heart, beyond the abstract
> Duty and respect, accorded a public monument.

The measured cadence and traditional diction of Anglo-Irish verse, however, characterize all of Montague's poetry in *Patriotic Suite* except for the last poem, a single couplet, in section seven: "Elegant port-wine brick, a colonial dream:/ *Now we own the cow, why keep the cream?*" The rude, homespun metaphor of the last line introduces the dramatic persona that Montague does so well and which, in fact, characterizes his best poetry.

"Annus Mirabilis, 1961" is generally colloquial in diction, though contemporary may be the more exact term, for reserve and control necessitate a traditional structure. The poem is a gentle ironic castigation of Ireland for belittling its revolutionary fathers. Spirit and freedom become unimportant in a state that measures its value in terms of "trade expansion" and neglects an intrinsic idea of self, one that has inspired revolutionary movements for hundreds of years.

"1966 and All That" stresses again the new complacence of Ireland in the midst of a much more energetic modern world. The poem ends by recalling the opening of *Patriotic Suite* from the point of view of someone who has spent some time, and some poems, examining modern Ireland: "the herring gull claims the air/ again, that note!/ above a self-drive car." Though he seems to lack optimism, Montague actually intends to make Ireland aware of its course, not to condemn it. Two quotations at the end indicate alternative paths: from Edmund Spenser, "They say it is the Fatal Destiny of that land that no purposes whatsoever which are meant for her good will prevail;" and from Engels, "The real aims of a Revolution, those which are not illusions, are always to be realized after that Revolution." We are left, then, to interpret these quotations as we will and apply them, again as we will, to Montague's portrayal of modern Ireland. Though only implicit here, such is the usual method of Montague's verse: to allow the personae or the scene to convey value. Clearly, we are to believe that the spirit which took Ireland from under the wing of Mother England can take her to dignity and strength, but only if the people do not allow themselves to be lulled into passivity by the new and minimal prosperity.

The insubstantiality of Ireland's new image becomes evident in *A New Siege*. The poem begins by announcing the cyclic appearance of the recalcitrant Irish spirit which was prophesied by the ending of

Patriotic Suite: "once again, it happens,/ like an old Troubles film,/ run for the last time. . . ." The references in this part of the poem are familiar even to people whose acquaintance with the history of Ireland is scant. But Montague's commitment to troubled Ulster in this poem necessitates his dealing with historical events that only a native or a specialist in Irish history would recognize at once. Exacting examination of *A New Siege* is necessary for one to comprehend the allusions, as has been shown by Serge Fauchereau's translation into French, published in *Esprit* (1971). The notes explain events, characters, and allusions. What Montague intended in this poem, though, was not simply a presentation of the history, legendary and factual, of Londonderry. He selected a city in Northern Ireland that has been for centuries identified with rebellion to illustrate the nature of the new rebellion. At the time the poem was written, the Catholics were mainly defensive, in a state of siege. Thus the earlier precedent of the siege of 1688-89, when the city held out successfully for 105 days, is reversed. The current siege is much longer, and no real hope of cessation is offered. In anticipation of this new condition, Montague did not project a victory which would be a copy of any past one. He envisions "a new order/ a new anarchy/ always different/ always the same."

The contention that the violence in Ulster is part of a wider process of change is repeated by Montague throughout the poem. In one stanza he cites the uprising on college campuses which occurred so often in America during the late 50s and through the 60s. But this poem remains tied closely to the North and closer

still to Londonderry, as seems stressed in Montague's
dedication of the poem to Bernadette Devlin with the
hopeful inscription: "Old moulds are broken in the
North."

The sound of the breaking mould has been heard in
rifle, grenade, and bomb. I await the sound of the new
and must pessimistically wonder if Ireland in general,
the North in particular, can escape the political lethargy
that followed partition. Only a solution to Irish violence
on categorically different grounds can, it seems to me,
assure a country that will have a cultural existence
which belongs to the present. The poets, especially, have
brought to Ireland news of change, of new joy and pain;
but the plain people of Ireland remain in the world of
the 1950 American swing and have not heeded often
enough their artists, the signalers of the process of man.
Violence sweeps over, as poets write in avant-garde
terms of radical solutions.

In particular, I must wonder if John Montague has
tied his talent to a culture that cannot respect it; to
wonder if his poetry would not be furthered by his total
rejection of Ireland, which he did not even do in the
50s. At least it is possible to observe that Montague's
poetry grows in technique as he increases in
vulnerability. In *The Rough Field,* especially *A New
Siege,* he risks much by believing contemporary Ireland
is worth writing about. Only the sound of a new,
peaceful order will prove him right.

8
Conclusion

John Montague's poems and stories from his first volume to his most recent one examine the family, the community, and the experiences that shaped the being we, and he, recognize as John Montague. This is not to place him among the undifferentiated mass of people who often seem to be gathering around the social sciences in an attempt to find a jargon and a few basic structures within which contemporary problems may be isolated. Montague's language has always been that of people: peasants, poets, intellectuals. Whoever finds a moment of coalescence of forces, or illustrates its absences, has concerned Montague. The variety of sounds and forms which are in his writing contain much of his strength, though critics have often been troubled by it. No one sound or form characterizes Montague's writing. The extremes of Montague's characters and personae provide an almost singular portrayal of life. Mythic patterns occur in Montague's writing, as they do in that of other important writers today, such as Thomas Kinsella, Gary Snyder, and David Jones.

Interestingly, none of these writers has adopted forms so important in contemporary British poetry which is based on rock music and the drug experience. Unlike Pete Brown and Anselm Hollo, for instance, all of these poets look for precedent in past cultures. Even Ginsberg and Snyder have chosen forms that are predicated by traditions that are centuries old.

The forms of poetry that have come from Manchester and Liverpool reflect a consciousness that is without nationality but which belongs to a culture that is recognizable and adhered to by multitudes. Often called simply "the movement," this culture is best embodied in the life styles and music of The Beatles. Though aware of these new forms and concepts, Montague has chosen a very different approach to life and art. Even in his lyrics he is often *engagé* but without the antiestablishment center of many writers today who posit a militantly alternative art. Montague, however, does oppose establishments that deny the freedom and rights of men. As Ginsberg has assessed the wrongs of American culture and celebrated life that is not chained, so Montague has done in his poems and stories about life in Northern Ireland, most noticeably in *The Rough Field.*

Perhaps all writers today must begin by examining themselves in a context that is broader than a single nation or culture. To discover the limits of self in a world with such mobility as exists today forces the writer, especially, to acknowledge an identity that is based on an understanding as general as a psychological study. The influence of Freud has, obviously, not run its course. Equally strong is the need to find a place, study its past, and believe in its future. Recognition of the importance of Ireland to him as man and writer continues from Montague's earliest writing to his latest. Legend, archaeology, history, and contemporary life all concern him; and their details become the manifestations of patterns which are universal and mythic for him.

What course Montague will take in the future is risky to predict. Montague's writing does not, of course, totally depend on the political situation of Northern Ireland. But by now it is clear he will try to remain involved. If the bloody violence continues without hope of settlement, the choice not only of Montague but of all concerned writers in Ireland and England must be to become more involved in working for what may well be a radical solution to an age-old problem or complete avoidance of the culture and society. In the case of John Montague, at least, the last choice does not seem a possible one.

Selected Bibliography

POETRY

All Legendary Obstacles. Dublin: Dolmen, 1966. 300 signed copies.

The Bread God. Dublin: Dolmen, 1968. 250 signed and numbered copies with 1-150 hors-commerce.

A Chosen Light. London: MacGibbon and Kee, 1967.

Forms of Exile. Dublin: Dolmen, 1958.

Home Again. Belfast: Belfast Publications, 1967.

Hymn to the New Omagh Road. Dublin: Pvt. Ptd. at Dolmen, 1968. 175 signed copies.

Patriotic Suite. Dublin: Dolmen, 1966. 1,000 copies with 100 signed and numbered.

Poisoned Lands and Other Poems. London: MacGibbon and Kee, 1961. Chester Springs: Dufour, 1963.

Tides. Dublin: Dolmen, 1971.

FICTION

Death of a Chieftain and Other Stories. London: MacGibbon and Kee, 1967. Chester Springs: Dufour, 1968.

EDITED WORKS

With Thomas Kinsella. *The Dolmen Miscellany of Irish Writing.* Dublin: Dolmen; London: Oxford University Press, 1962.

With Liam Miller. *A Tribute to Austin Clarke on his Seventieth Birthday, 9 May 1966.* Dublin: Dolmen, 1966.